Leaves On Pages

John Grey

Contents

TOUGH

Another day in the desert. Not a cloud in the sky.
No songbirds. Just vultures. Not a tree. But here and there,
stunted grass. Wildlife is mostly lizards, snakes, the occasional
jack-rabbit with ears tall and lean enough to give their heads away.

And life is always in the distance. Is that a train? And are those
trucks on the horizon? And mountains? Always a reminder that
life is elsewhere, height likewise. Yet this is where people make
their homes.
A shack. A cottage. Even welcome mats to wipe those dusty boots.
And the phone lines may be thin as thread but they're there,
humming in the sky. Throats aren't parched enough that they
can't talk.

But no cloud in that sky. Didn't know until now how threatening
blue could be. And the sun just does what it's told, by God or the
old codger who runs the gas station near Clifford. Blister. Melt.
Desiccate. Burn that pale white flesh until it stings.

But I remember the bitter New England winters too. A different
kind of torture. I'm starting to realize you have to hate where you live.
And it's good to be around folks you despise, who despise you.
I drink up my own complaints like water whereas once I used
to toss them like logs, set a fire to roaring. For, after a while, Eden
would drive a man nuts. Too calm. Too pure. Too safe. Too
comfortable.
A snake with an apple indeed. No, give me a snake with a rattle.

WRITING A CHECK OUT FOR MY WIFE

My signature begins with good intentions
but is unintelligible by name's end.
Yes, it's a scrawl.
Some handwriting interpreter
could probably concoct
inalienable truths
in the way the "J" swallows the "o",
the "G" is never the same twice,
the "y" fades too quickly.
Maybe, some politician, priest,
ex-lover, would make meat of the fact
that it's the left hand that did it.
But if you trace the check back
through the writing to the pen
to the fingers to the man
who filled it out for you,
it should become clearer.
I give you twenty dollars
like I give you love.
So the word in my head
can fall apart on the paper.
So the neat heart
can make a mess of it.

FRIDGE MAGNETS

Your fridge is attached to
a grocery list,
the local council's rules
for garbage day,
the cast of Star Trek,
your niece's baby,
and a reminder that
your cousin's birthday
is the twenty fourth.
Your kitchen's size
accommodates the fridge.
Your house is big enough
to have a kitchen.
The neighborhood
has space enough
for your house to fit.
And where would the city be
without your neighborhood,
or the state without your city,
your country without your state,
the world without your country.
And then there's the solar system,
the sun flaring up again,
cooking world, country,
state, city, neighborhood,
house, even the kitchen
where, to the refrigerator door,
you fasten a note to yourself,
"buy sunscreen."

A WALK ALONG A NANTUCKET BEACH

Everything pulls apart and forms again,
from wave to sand to gull flock.
Crash and hiss and shriek,
the sounds of severing, stitching.
I don't even have to walk the beach,
collect shells, dangle toes in water.
This world could exist as a noise
and that would be enough.

Along the shore, every shard is
the mouthpiece for something, dead or living.
The driftwood tells of boats,
the brittle bones, of sharks.
Only the ocean is mute, a constant
reshuffle of despair and triumph,
immense plates of water, foam,
sliding across each other.
It is all the stories, all of the time,
but none of the telling.

But then there's more clatter, like
this beach never stops happening.
Breakers slap against cliff
then cascade back down.
Sanderlings pry open their salty lunchbox.
A dog scampers in and out of the swell,
brings loud, yapping anarchy
to the break and heal of form.

I wonder if I'm the dog in this picture,
let loose like the wind?
Or am I the remnants, one more slab of alabaster,
pearl, ragged cowrie, shiny stone?
I grab a handful of sand
and the grains escape through my fingers,
invite me to follow.
Am I just one more of them?
The sky hovers over it all
like a great blue forehead stuck in that thought.

HOW THE OTHER HALF LIVES

Rita is much too much.
She lives in a house that's
twice the size of ours.
It is still only half as big
as her delusions of grandeur.
And her husband's a doctor and I'm not.
Handy for her, I guess,
for if looks can kill,
she likely needs a man of medicine nearby.
Rita has her eyes on the prize
which, from what I've heard,
is to purchase the place next door,
knock down the old Victorian of course,
put up a snazzy guest house.
Any day now, her husband will be
named head of the hospital.
What's to stop her buying up the neighborhood.
Yes, she dresses well, if by 'well' you mean expensive.
And that car she drives is exceeded only by
the other car in which she's driven around.
Her finger boasts a giant diamond.
And such a tiny little gem on yours.
Oh well, why don't you just roll over
and I'll hug you.
My understanding is that waists
we all come with, likewise arms and hands.
I guarantee that, at this moment,
Rita's not being held any tighter than you.
And I'm kissing the small of your back.
Does Rita have the small of anything?

THE NAME

There should be a name for people
who sit on a rock for hours
and just stare at the sea.
Land's end becomes worries' end.
Lives are nothing more
than horizon shimmer,
seagull uproar,
the flop of wave on sand.
And forget conversing with people.
Conversation flaps its sails,
glides through the laughing foam.

There should be name for people
whose brown eyes
succumb to blue reflection,
whose feet dangle
the heaviest weight they know,
nothing but light between them
and the sun.

There should be a name for people
seduced by brightness,
the rollicking ebb and flow,
who construct all that there need be
from a sea-breeze,
who really do believe
that, even with eyes closed,
the sound is vision enough,

the world breathes water.
There should be a name for such people.

But if there's not,
give them my name.

STATIONARY

From his bedroom,
he could hear the trains in the distance
but the hills blocked the view.

They didn't stop.
That sound went
as quickly as it came.

As he lay atop the sheets,
he could only imagine that locomotive,
its passenger cars
or tankers or crates of goods
on flatbeds.

And they were going places.
He sure wasn't.

From his bedroom,
he could also hear his parents
in the kitchen or the parlor,
arguing as usual.

It came as silence.
It went as silence.
But, in between, the noise
pulled up and stayed.

As he lay atop the sheets,
the room shook from the shouting below.

He closed his eyes,
tensed his body.
He was waiting for a train.

ONE DROP OF RAIN

The lizard tried to snare it
with quicksilver tongue
as if it were a cricket.
The toad lurched forward,
attempted to trap it on its scaly back.
The rattlesnake suddenly uncoiled
as if tapped on the shoulder.
The jackrabbit jumped
through its glistening hoop.
The puma purred.
The startled scorpion scattered.
Pipe organ cactus pleaded
with every bristle.
The saguaro held out its beggar hand
but was denied.
Finally, the heat, the earth,
divided it in two,
none for each.

BUT YOU KNOW THIS ALREADY

There's a love that shops, that irons,
that makes the beds and washes dishes,
walks the dog in the morning,
that can cook and tend to the sick,
does laundry and takes out the trash,
even adjusts the day for the latter
when a holiday falls on the Monday.

There's a love that keeps up the insurance payments
for house and car, that pays the gas bill on time,
and has never forgotten a birthday or an anniversary,
that donates unneeded clothing to charity
and puts money away for replacement windows.

There's a love that flops down before the TV
or summarizes the day, good or bad,
over a dinner table, and is unafraid
to work the plunger on an uncooperative toilet
or scrub a wall free of stains.

There's a love that feels so inevitable
you can set your watch by it,
take your pain, your sorrow to its source

and emerge glad and healed,
that will always be there,
even when nothing else is.

But please, just once, spare me that love.
Give me the grand passion.

THE INTERNET AGE BEGINS

Nobody goes door to door anymore.
Nobody drives through every small town in the state
with a suitcase full of samples
and a spiel drummed into him
by the fat guy at head office
with the taste for cheap cigars.

Hasn't been a one since they found Tom Herkel
in that motel outside Wichita,
flat on his back, unblinking eyes
staring at the ceiling's octopus-shaped water stain.
His tongue was the last to sprout
"You really need this cleanser."
His hands were the last to squeeze
that green liquid onto the brown patch on a rug.

Nobody drives a battered Ford,
thinking "Today's the day, I make
my biggest sale ever."
Nobody, late at night,
pulls over into the parking lot
of a cheap motel,
barely enough strength left
to curse what a man must do
to make a living.

The maid found him.
She had no clue he was the last.
She just figured him for the latest.

THE WOMAN ON THE SUBWAY

She's on the Red Line,
no doubt headed for the ratified air
of Harvard Square.
Her nails are painted green
but freshly bitten.
She fiddles with the brown ringlet
that won't leave her eyes alone.
A stuffed backpack
is her only companion.
She's wearing some kind of perfume
that I can't decipher
and a gray woolen skirt
that rests politely on her knees.
She doesn't look in my direction.
They never do.
And, even if she did,
I'm much too shy to smile.
And certainly saying "hello"
is out of the question.
I drop my head into my book,
scan a paragraph,
then look up again,
repeat this exercise for five stops.
She is one more
that I would like to know
but never will.
I live in a world
of opportunities lost,
risks not taken.
It even has its own transport system.

MATT MUGGED

Matt just happened to be in the wrong place at the wrong time
that's all.
Of course, late night in the city is always wrong on both counts.
Like when the clubs let out and everybody's strutting or staggering
to the backstreet where they parked their car.
Matt discovered that a crowd can become a man alone
without him even thinking about it.
The clubbers go their own way. None of them are Matt's.
And there's always guys hanging out that you don't want to mess with.
Mostly gangs. But sometimes, if he's big and brawny enough,
or wielding a Glock, just the one.
It was three brutes who came at Matt.
One grabbed Matt's arms, wrenched them behind his back,
the second slapped him across the face,
the third rifled his pockets, grabbed his wallet, his phone,
then snatched his watch from his wrist for good measure.
They took a good look at Matt's shoes but then shook their heads.
He didn't know whether to feel relieved or insulted.
Then they shoved him down to the sidewalk and ran off.
At least, they left him his car-keys.
He drove home in pain, in embarrassment, in anger.
Spent an hour cancelling credit cards, his phone number,
before crawling into bed. Matt didn't sleep so well.
There are times when even a soft, comfy mattress
can be the wrong place at the wrong time.
Like when thoughts converge from out of the darkness,
and there's three of them to only the one doing the thinking.
One thought grabs his arms. The second slaps his face.
The third takes just about everything he has on him.

But not the shoes. At least not the shoes.
Those shoes are lying at the foot of the closet where he tossed them.
Lucky, they didn't take the damn things, he reckons.
For what would he cancel? His shoes or his feet?

OF NATURE AND NURTURE

My serious eldest sister left home
to work as a governess in the outback.

The wild youngest settled down eventually,
married an Irish cop.

The one in the middle dated sports stars
before getting wed to a plumber.

I was hardly even me yet
and they were already out of the house,

their futures blinkered.
My father was dead.

My mother worked on hands and knees,
eking out as much overtime

as her scrubbing brush could get.
This was what I had to work with

along with radio, TV, books
and, of course, school.

What I'm thinking now,
what I'm feeling now,

are the effect of these causes.
It's not a straight encouraging line.

My solitude is in there somewhere.

WHEN SINATRA DIED

That same evening,
I found a dead songbird,
called it Sinatra,
as the moon cocked its hat,
here and elsewhere
on a hazy twilight,
one more time for song
to throw up its hands
or drop to its knees -

I was deep in my Rat Pack phase,
the internet too young then
to care much for the old,
but the bobbysoxers got it,
to scratchy copies of "Songs For Swinging Lovers",
they lifted flat voices,
drowned out the echo of their teenage years –

mid-May, I was eyeballing the TV,
lazy brown dog at my heels,
saw clip after clip of a dead alpha male
singing from black and white to color,
a chain of hits, every note covered,
from rubber tree plants
to fill 'em up Joe
and all the way –

out here on the avenue,
the songbirds are back,

new dog thinks he's hot
in a red bandana,
howls his own torch song
to whoever might hear,
all these years later,
I call him Sinatra,
the chairman of the board –

I've got visitors
with kids who weren't born
when Frankie was alive,
with their own heroes,
their own dead birds,
a love they may even yet
grow old enough to mourn.

INSOMNIA

Yes, I'd rather be in a sublime state of nothingness
but I am lying down, head propped on pillow,
reading Goethe with tears in my eyes.
And I'm imagining labyrinthine windings.
And wall panels that could be doors to secret passageways
or maybe they're not.
It is two in the morning and I can't sleep.
I'm untidy. A plane wreck. Can't find the black box.
And young Werther merely confirms that life's a bitch.
As if that needs confirming.
I wish I knew how to forge a new identity.
But my power has been vastly exaggerated.
By me most of all.
At least my wife can dream through all this.
She is not under the bed-lamp, bombed by light.
Her fantasies have taken her over completely.
My body has been preserved in this waxy reality.
And my brain is perusing powerful memory,
the kind that gets my present situation in so much trouble.
The night is not time off for me.
It's merely a relentless accumulation of incidents and ideas.
It's administered by Washington, a dead father,
and a long line of serious authors, also now dead.
I try to find a place for myself but all I can contribute
is this endless, unspoken commentary.
That's the problem. I try to approximate something.
I just can't accept the accidental nature of being.
And I'm up to the point where Werther shoots himself in the head.
This sturm und drang is all too much for me.

Maybe I should just take a pill.
I bought a bottle from the pharmacy for such an occasion.
But I fear chemicals.
I'm not sure they have my best interests at heart.
So I'll go on reading until my eyelids can take it no more.
And I'll see the protagonist through to the end.
If he's Werther, there's a funeral.
If he's me, sleep at last.

EVERGLADE SUNSET

egrets coiffed by white feathery fading sun,
steps as weightless as the mangrove island itself,
its drifting roots shaped like twisted arches -

levitating pastures, breeze-perfumed heat and mud,
skeletal lighthouse overgrown with vines,
buzzing insects living on their nerves -

not a heaven an angel would choose,
but a gator slinks through the brackish glare,
a passage into night, strongly worded

A BOOK FOR NO GOOD REASON

I buy a book by an author I've never heard of,
because the dust jacket is intact,
the cover, a picture of a girl
who's retained her girlhood over eighty years at least.
bent over, labelling leaves
with a couple of eager young helpers.

This is surely a novel where nothing much happens -
no sex. no violence - merely the care it takes
to paste woodland finds onto a blank notebook page,
label them with her best guess,
and now those leaves are mine.
whether maple or black birch,
they've passed through her hands
and now it's up to me to sort them out.

Yes. it's been eighty years
judging by the signature and date
scribbled on the dedication page,
a heroine who never grew old enough for heartbreak,
who adored the gentle rain
and the crackling of leaves and paper.
At the end of the book.
there is no going on for her,
merely back to the beginning.

Almost a century of folding linens.
of hanging Christmas decorations.
of picking apples.

learning to spell under the crotchety eye
of the town's spinster teacher.
If she's on her knees.
it's to give the floor a good scouring.
She only broaches death
when a baby sparrow dies in her palm.

Her world extends from woods to house
to fields to sagging barn.
She's seldom amazed
but never bored.
There's always another leaf,
there's always another wagon trundling by.
She knows beauty, more steady than spectacular,
the kind that can show up
at a yard sale later,
be worth no more than a dollar.
There she is, amid the weeping romances
and thunderous boys' adventure tales,
no suitors, no threats,
just a buyer who admires the cover,
gently turns the fragile pages,
buys it for no good reason,
at least, no better reason
than pasting leaves on pages.

EDISON'S BULB

Edison often put brainwaves to good use.
Like a light for the everyday.
A bulb same as this one above me.
It casts an even glow.
The lilacs come up purple not white.
The spines on the bookshelf are eminently readable.
I can even make out the dust on the computer screen.

I wonder what it would be like
to create something so perfect in its usefulness.
How rewarding for body and mind.
And what a comfort, even in old age,
to reach over the edge of the hospital bed
and flick on the wonders
of your youthful imagination.

Edison must have looked at the sun
and said to himself,
"I can make one of those."
And, as a byproduct, I can raise mankind
out of a kind of darkness
that's not fully covered by church sermons.

I'm sure there were many equations involved.
And brow-tapping.
And stacks of intellectual dominoes
that just didn't fall right.
Plus, he could have been sidetracked –

why not a patchwork quilt that doesn't unthread
instead of this electric light crap?

But he must have foreseen me reading
under a bed-lamp.
Or having to find something in the gloomiest corners
of a room.
And those camping trips with my father
when a fire informed what we were eating
but couldn't peer into the brushes,
pick out green eyes peering back.

True, light is not without its gruesome incidents.
Guy electrocuted on a pole.
Bulbs popping from a dripping ceiling.
Or me stumbling off a chair
as I try to replace one with burnt-out filament.
And there's that funeral light,
dimmed to imitate death
in a way that total blackness cannot.
And the streetlamps
that strangers gather mysteriously beneath.

But I'll take the downside.
Even its limitations.
Like, no matter how bright,
it cannot replicate day.

I'll even use it as a metaphor.
Like the bulb that pops into the head
as thought becomes idea.
Which makes me wonder
what popped into Edison's head

when he first came up with
the concept of artificial lightning.
Was it a bulb?
Was that cheating?

MISSISSIPPI

Don't think.
Just get through.
Place no trust in windowless houses.
Don't die on a sweaty day
in an uncomfortable chair
in the common room
of a ratty residential hotel.
When alone, breathe deeply.
When with people, compress.
Sit on a porch,
keep the stars company
or, if not, the rain.
Never go without water.
Just don't get your heart wet.
Remember always to wear something
that protects the soles of the feet.
Like a bus ticket, for example.
Squeeze rolls of paper towels
whenever the opportunity arises.
Swat mosquitoes before they slake their thirst.
Don't remind yourself how many times you've failed.
Take a lover even if he or she doesn't exist.
Don't take a bend in the road lightly.
Keep in mind that every roof leaks.
Don't let rancid smells prevent you from sleeping.
Disregard the children darting about like chickens.
Join in the throng when they envy the dead.
Ignore murder mysteries.
And box scores. And open palms.

But not food wagons.
Appreciate applause when you get it.
Don't go all fragile when you don't.
Treat sorrow like a benign child.
And don't bother waiting for an invitation from the rich.
And stay away from factories with ear-piercing machines.
Don't bitch but don't hug either.
Or drive after midnight.
Or make eye-contact with chain gangs.
You'll get by.
I did.
Find your place in line.
Fill out an application.
Work in shifts.
Go shirtless only if there's holes that need digging.

RAILROAD MAN

The railroad gives a history lesson and it's bitter –
spikes like the rusting bones of your body,
tie plates not connected to any other

and help that will never get here –
the land gave up everything
for the crossties, the sleepers, to dig themselves in -

it staked the horizon on parallel steel lines
that are already an inscription for a headstone
where only weeds find a use for the ballast -

once this track and you were going somewhere together -
the old Puffing Billy out of Junction City,
the old puffing man in the parlor with his pipe.

IT'S UP TO YOU

Wait for it -
here it comes out of me,
the tremors of timeless sorrow

with malice toward me
with charity for you

yes, from my side of things,
a kind of all-encompassing regret

a shameful face
applying for your good graces

not justice, not necessarily truth -

I'd be happy with your head's
reappearance on my pillow

and to be beloved in life –

well, that's how some
of us would put it -

those who've sat here
for the longest time
criminalizing themselves -

and, to stay with the vernacular,
it's not commuting of the sentence
I beg for -

just forgive me, please -

do yourself a great disservice

A 7 FOR PAIN

It's just pain.
It varies by degrees
but no other name for it will do.
I have ways of preventing it.
Some work. Some don't.
Some invoke other pains.
There are pills.
There are exercises.
There are even abstentions.
As a last resort of course.
There are some I can live with.
Some I can't.
But I love with both kinds.
None are terminal.
None cry out
for a week or two in a hospital bed.
Sometimes rubbing helps.
Sometimes rubbing
by someone I love
helps so much more.
And pain can come from anywhere.
Like handling roses
and being pricked by thorns.
Or falling hard on the sidewalk
and scalping a kneecap.
Of course, emotional pain
is another matter entirely.
But when it leads to physical pain…

see the comment regarding rubbing
      above.
The doctor often asks me
to quantify the pain
on a scale of one to ten.
I inevitably say 7.
That's the number I figure
will get me immediate help
but not send my poor body
for a series of tests.
I can live with 7
whether or not it's really a 10
or a 4.
I'm alive, aren't I.
That's a 7 right there.

ANDY'S DONE FOR THE NIGHT

Softly, next to an overfilled trash can, Andy the guitarist,
tired from another night replaying his life as a failed musician,
sits and counts the coins in his cap, then shoves
them in his pocket, looks back on twenty years
of small change and indifferent audiences.
His brother Tim is an engineer, has a well-paid job,
one that took him far from home but closer
to their father. In the house on Claymore, the old
man attends to his roses when he's not polishing the glass
that protects Tim's graduation picture. Nothing
on the mantel of the long-haired Eric Clapton wannabe
who strummed and plucked his battered third-hand Fender
in the bedroom, various amateur nights, then in the park,
on the street. The old man only has two sons. If it wasn't
for Andy, they'd have all done brilliantly.

A GERMAN MOTHER'S WARNING

How could you marry a man
who propounded the third law
of thermodynamics?

What if the steaming coffee
yon put before him
interrupted his train of thought
and he cursed you

or if the heat and the cup
actually inspired his equation
and he gave you no credit?

Could you live with sex
that explained nothing
of the behavior of electrolytes
in the presence of electric currents?

Imagine being polarized
by polarization
or, with bucket and pail in hand,
standing between him
and absolute zero.

Steer clear of all who would
explain the universe
You'll be consumed by his formula
or, at best, everything will fit it
but you

I COULD WRITE ANOTHER HUNDRED POEMS JUST LIKE THIS

A woman is
the gratitude for
your own happiness.
She is Port Chester
in fog.
Not forgetting
a rare October snowfall
and, of course,
a podium suddenly
emptied of its speaker,
or a body that turns
up on a beach
miles from where it drowned.
A woman is the
buffing and polishing,
and maybe a tourist
in sun-glasses and shorts.
And yes she is basil
sprinkled lightly on everything,
and what's ever in your hands
when the folks are coming over.
A woman is headlines, small print,
daisies, roses, weeds.
She is the Cadillac parked outside
in the rain.
And the rain, of course,
pinging on the metal.
She's what's been around so long

it must be worth something.
Bui, of course,
only she can cash it in.

STEEPLECHASE

There's fence
and there's fence
with bay mare leaping,
neck stretched,
hoofs hooked under.

There's brick wall
and there's brick wall
with hock elastic,
head risen,
breast extended,
horse jumping clear.

There's morning
where sun delineates
the features of the field,
separates fence from grasses,
wall from trees.

And there's morning
when saddle grips muscle
hands slap speed from reins.

There's a time of dream,
laid out, enticing.
There's a time of dream,
stallion, rider, and coming true.

FOREIGN CANDY

The candy tasted like burnt tar.
His little sister ate it
in the passenger seat of his car
as they drove through town.

He named all the stores he passed by.
That's what soldiers do, he said.
It's how you know you remember them.

He stopped for squabbling pigeons on the road.
As feral as rats they may have been
but they were his birds.
He wasn't about to skittle them.

It was battle-zone candy, he told her.
She screwed up her face but she finished it.
Besides he added, I had to bring back something

The taste stayed with her for days.
She got off easy as it turns out.

MENTAL CONSTRUCT

Objective reality is now mental construct,
and context is intentional if truth hangs
on meaning and not just references. I'm over
legal positivism. But contrary reasoning? Sign me up.

For me, skepticism makes great wall-paper.
And morals are raked up with November leaves.
My neighborhood can be the Master Argument for all I care.
I'm past truth. I'm nibbling on the proposition.

The difference between motive and motivation
is sea-weed and sand but I don't take to the water.
I'm here, dicing and slicing pessimism,
toasting optimism, buttering it, smothering it with jam.

I'm pragmatic says my old school master.
I'm a child, my ex-lover retorts. A formula is satisfied
by values. I enjoy pigging out on chicken wings,
F Scott Fitzgerald and walks by the canal.

It's morning. I'm reading up on drive-by shootings.
A car could bear a sniper. Should I be surprised?
Could be a priest in there forgiving me my sins.
With a bullet to the head no less. Carry on neural correlations.

REGARDING THE FACTS OF LIFE

Jack was ten, witnessing
an enforced calf birth.
His father reached into the womb,
untangled limbs, moved the stomach
this way, that way, found the hooves
and chained them.

With much grunting,
and Jack's tiny hands joining in,
farmer George jerked the chain taut
and pulled like it was a tug of war
between one fifty pounds of experience
and half a ton of dumb usefulness.

Outside, the weather blew a near blizzard.
The barn shook, bitter cold
permeated the straw-laden nursery.
Rough shivering fingers, cloudy grunts –
the tiny creature roughed and tore its way
along the birth canal,
before finally popping free
in a cascade of leg and cries
and ruptured sack and water and freezing blood.

The mother turned her head,
shrugged off the pain,
began licking the newborn,
afterbirth flopping against the back of her legs.
The baby licked in return,

stumbled to its feet through a dozen falls,
attached itself to a teat.

Mother unharmed, calf healthy,
and the almighty dollar,
also unharmed and healthy.
Money on the hoof,
was George's favorite saying.

Two years later, George handed Jack a book,
talked to him a little about love and marriage,
sex and childbirth, all in an embarrassed whisper.
So other details came to light.
The cow was only half the story.

ONE HUNDRED ROOMS

She sits in her car in the parking lot
of the motel, can't be sure which room
her cheating husband occupies.
Maybe he's in all one hundred rooms
with one hundred different lovers.

She tries to compare a woman
she's never seen to the face that
looks back at her in the rear-view mirror.
Who wins the prize for the prettiest eyes?
The most alluring mouth?

And what of her shape?
Who is the most hour-glass?
Who the most vase?
It's the sheer novelty she knows
she loses out on.
Ten years they've been together.
So many times, situations good and bad,
she can remember.
Novelty doesn't even keep a record.

There are plenty of cars in that lot
but only one is occupied,
only one woman is slumped over
a steering wheel,
pondering her next move.
Burst in on them?
All one hundred rooms?

Or go home?

Just the one house.

She always figured one would be enough.

ANNA AND THE MAGIC ACT

You felt for his female assistant,
thin and vulnerable,
naked but for
the sparkle of her sequins.
When Mephisto sawed the woman in half,
you shuddered.
When she slipped into the trunk,
you felt each sword
he jammed right through its sides.
And when, with a snap of his fingers,
the woman vanished into thin air,
you sensed the depths
of her invisibility,
still so manifest
even when he brought her back.

THE MARE AND THE STORM

I strolled through the alfalfa field
circled by panicked insects
and with a storm slowly making something
of the warm, too peaceful, air.

The mare in a nearby field
proved the perfect weather forecaster.
She galloped then stopped, galloped and stopped,
before neighing as loud as the thunder to come.

I made my way through a gnat cloud
to the fence, leaned over,
tried my best to calm her.
But her head wasn't into hearing.

The bridle hung at my side.
It was time to bring her in to the safety of the barn.
But she pounded her hooves,
swung her head like a weapon at a buzzing fly.

Luckily, lightning brought her to her senses.
It lit up the afternoon like a sign from the god of equines.
She stopped and shuddered at the distant thunder.
I slipped through the gate and rubbed her neck,

threaded her mane with my fingers.
Slowly but surely, I became bigger to her
than the dark clouds moving in,
the next flash, that even closer rumble.

I walked her as confidently as I could
as the air grew gloomier and even the bugs
began to dart here and there,
looking for a hideaway to ride out the storm.

"Everything's ok," was my mantra.
I hoped it would be hers as well.
She clip-clopped gently up the trail
even as the sky closed in all around us.

We made it to the barn, the stall,
just as those clouds burst and rain plummeted down.
She kissed my cheek to thank me for my timing,
or perhaps even my power over the heavens.

I was mightier than the god of all the horses.
And I had sugar cubes in my pocket.
Her tongue snared one, then two, then three,
I was the supreme being, these the objects of her faith.

A LONG TIME

Life is good sometimes
but there's these long, long periods
between when last it was
and when it's going to be the next time.

Imagine walking to the moon.
Or watching Andy Warhol's "Empire"
ten thousand times over.
Or having to read every blog
on the internet.

Longer than it'd take
to pay off a dozen mortgages.
Or a teenager
stares in the mirror.
Or a stone house stands.
Or finding a word
to rhyme with guru.

Imagine modernism
finally growing old
or the newly constructed
being taken down at last.
Or trying\to calculate
the number of pigeons
that have ever lived.

Life is good sometimes
but it's mostly mediocre,

When it gets good again,
babies born this very day
could well be in their forties.
Forty years of age
or forty hand-made string ornaments,
I cannot say.

GETTING AT THE LAST KETCHUP IN THE BOTTLE

Thumb can't reach.
The fork and spoon
just won't fit through
the bottle's narrow neck.
I slap my hand against
the Heinz sticker
but nothing inside shakes loose.
I could tip it upside down
but, when it comes to ketchup,
gravity takes its time.
The easiest thing
would be toss this
bottle in the trash
and open a new one.
But who writes a poem
about the easiest thing?

GREAT BLUE HERON

The great blue heron is more wary
than terrified.
It knows I'm there.
But it doesn't dart into the nearest bush.
Nor let out a cry
to warn all others of its kind
of my presence.
But its shoreline stalking slows,
neck tightens,
head slowly turns in my direction.

The bird's feathered crown rises.
Wings lift and spread.
Talons let go the surface.
It lifts gracefully to the bough
of a nearby oak.

No way the heron will abandon
its feeding ground
to my presence.
It will wait me out.
Besides, the fish in that brown-skinned pond
are not going anywhere.
It knows me for an interloper,
that I have other places to go
for my succor, my survival.

As I turn and walk away,
I hear it floating down behind me.
Mine is a heavy roughshod gait.
The forest favors soft landings.

MEET ME

By the clock tower.
Seven p.m.
When the crickets are like so many
clicking, clacking, chirring tongues.
And the grass is dark,
the church wall slightly moonstruck.
I'm the one with the beard
and a faint pink tinge
to the roof of my mouth.
I'll be translating the passersby by
into you, maybe you
and definitely not you.
And I may be singing under my breath.
I must confess this is all new to me.
I typically meet people
in stages, from their name
to their looks, to their thoughts,
to their feelings.
And here's a situation
when they could all come at me
at once.
Yes, by the clock tower.
There's only one clock tower.
Seven p.m.
There's only one seven p.m.
My knees will be pale
but you won't know that
and my teeth could go
on a chattering binge.

Even when it's not so cold.
I'll try to smolder
but I don't guarantee it.
And be prepared for a confidence
that could shrink before your eyes.
I've never done this sort of thing before.
The clock tower is an old hand.
Three hands actually.
And 7.00 p.m. has been early evening
for so many couples before us.
But I'll be there.
A famous landmark.
A familiar time.
Everything not famous or familiar
will be me.

THE WHITMAN TRAIL

I'm back in Brooklyn, walking the streets late at night, can never
escape from the fact that Walt Whitman trod these very side-
walks,
strolled up the heights, looked over the water to the bustling city
beyond.
I'm thirsty for company but coffee will have to do, a small oasis
in the dark, a few tables, chairs where Walt might have sat,
a pretty girl behind the counter whose great great grandmother
could have even smiled at Whitman as she took his money.
And the customers are young, their poems spread across the
table-tops,
sharing this week's anguish with their peers.
Budding Whitmans. Wannabe Whitmans. Never-will-be
Whitmans.
Coffee's from the Kona Coast. Sips like short sentences. Tasty.
Much depth.
Probably didn't have the myriad of choices back in Walt's day.
Couldn't taste Brazil or southeast Asia or Hawaii on a whim.
Besides, back then the war was fought near, not far away in
deserts.
I'm back in Brooklyn and every moment is a moment in the
bard's life.
I look in the window of a bookstore. There's Grisham and
Ludlum and Whitman.
I see a young boy reading something by the light of a third floor
window.
Whitman, I'm sure. The wind picks up. To flutter the leaves of
grass, no doubt.

SWISS MONKS

At the edge of a lake
stands an abandoned monastery.
"Hasn't been occupied for more
than a hundred years," says the guide.
Despite the crumbling outer walls
and the encroaching vegetation,
its facade retains a certain school principal sternness.

These monks apparently
were the most zealous of religious hermits,
hidden away even from each other
in their tunics and cowls,
sequestered most hours in cold, damp unadorned cells.

"They ate no animal flesh," the guide advises us,
nor fish, nor even eggs.
What little sleep they managed was on beds of straw.
Every midnight, they rose for mass
while days were spent in labor or reading or prayer.
And most curious of all, they uttered not a sound.
All were totally mute."
They must have been such a forbidding brotherhood
as they passed their uninviting lives
within the walls of that prison by another name.

The lake water's patina is a glistening blue
and the valley is like a Constable watercolor.
Lush, forested hills surround the decaying cloister
and the river grass sings as much as the flocks of birds do.

If their piety sought the meaning of life,
maybe it should have looked out a window occasionally.
And if their silence was a tuning fork
longing to hum with the word of God,
then surely, in these bountiful surrounds,
He didn't just speak but chattered constantly.
The abbey remains a testimony to those
who would not see nor hear.
Or a crumbling cenotaph
for those who do not need one.

A RAINY DAY IN SUBURBIA

There are days
in which every moment
seems like an episode in rerun,
like when she says how much she loves the rain
or any other aspect of our lives
when seen through a bedroom window.

Bored with the news.
blocking out a father who suffers from early onset dementia,
an American western princess –
I haven't the heart to tell her it's not just rain.

This is our soap opera,
every hour is derivative of every other hour,
each Thursday is actually Tuesday,
in fact, everything is the one thing,
as predictable as it is unnerving,
as forgotten as it is forgiven.

And yes, that is rain,
but it's also metaphors for her eyes and open mouth,
as she lives this bland sitcom,
with its breaks for advertising –
coffee mostly, occasionally wine.

There's a laugh track for the names
her sisters call their children.
And another for her brother's embrace of –
what is it this week? Zen Buddhism.

And of course, no bigger guffaw
than when, for the hundredth time this year
she says, "I think I might join the gym."
When it stops raining that is.

She could work on her modest anxiety,
her recalcitrant transformations.
It's raining hard now.
This is a marathon of sorts.
It plays into some negative emotions
like we'll never have kids of our own
to curse with funny names.
Or why don't I join the gym
so we can do something together.

The rain seems fully aware of ordinary lives.
It has it on good authority of the gray clouds overhead
that no billionaire celebrities live here.

It harps on our predictability,
a rainy day spent everywhere but in bed.
It explodes on our nothingness,
has known homeless people with more of a home
than what we present to the world.

She reckons she's being unrealistic
but she likes Sarah for a girl, Matthew for a boy.
It's what she says every day.
And it goes quickly into syndication.

POETRY – NOT EVEN A MISDEMEANOR

The fact is,
no matter who's in charge,
no one's about to lock me up
for the poetry I write.
Criticizing the powers that be
is a national birthright
that becomes a ritual in time
and finally, a doctrine.
Poetry is merely more fodder
for deaf ears.

Oh there's a passion here all right,
a determination to get down on paper
where it hurts the most.
But nobody is after the literary vote.
And poets don't head any lists
of possible donors.

This is not South America.
Or Nazi Germany.
Or the Soviet Union.
No one comes for poets in the night.
And none of us spend years in prison
writing diatribes in our own blood.
No, we save that blood for our best metaphors.

I just can't imagine a world
where readings are broken up by soldiers,

chapbooks are passed around surreptitiously
like drugs.
In America,
no poets appear on wanted posters.
Now unwanted posters…
that's a different story.

FOR YOUR VIEWING PLEASURE, EX-TINCTION

Twenty years ago, maybe once a week,
I would have heard the warning...
Wild Kingdom, a khakied guest on Johnny Carson.
Now there's channels that will pop
a dirty white explorer's hat atop my head 24/7.
No rifle shoved into my hand of course
but a digital video camera with telescopic lens.
They'll shunt me off to some place
in the dwindling wilds of Africa
where I can only see some beast or another.
My eyes feel a creature's prickly surface,
rub another's armor skin.
I can walk in their deep footprints,
dig in scat like a child in a sand-pit.
I know the gestation period of an elephant
better than my wife's.
I've learned what foliage giraffes prefer,
been witness to lions leaping on
the backs of antelopes and zebras.
Always they end with maps of disappearing
rain-forest, savannah, ancient forest.
Not a comfort to the one
who feels the love shrink day by day,
the respect atrophy, the job become
no more than a paid means to its end.
Everything's endangered
and I thought it was just me.

The sub-text of everything is extinction.
In my life, beasts I never knew existed
    don't.

GRASSLANDS

It's calm here now but once this was
all ash, the sizzling gift of a volcano
like a star rising from the crater
and crashing to the earth below.
It took a lot of rain to festoon
these plains with their grasses,
a hundred thousand mine-loads of minerals
to work all of that scorching and burning
into something soft and giving.
Sometimes, when there's just a
breath of wind, the rustle of the
grass is like a whispering,
an unforced remembering in the
thinnest of it, back to the day
when it first called itself a meadow,
and beyond that when the land
bedded down with the eruption.
It's in the animals as well,
in that pause between mouthfuls,
when they trail their own smells
back to the first sniff that
wasn't of fire, to that first spring,
when they first fed well on the
succulent green fields despite
a horizon of receding orange-red,
of forbidding cloud and sinuous lightning.
But even in the beasts, there's
a recollection of wild bodies that knew fire,
that scrambled over or stumbled through

the searing heat, that burst into flame,
until one was cool enough and whole enough
to go on feeding.
In each blade, each lowed head,
there's an explosion and a strafing,
a raging fire and an internal heat.
But in the eye of it all,
there's that calm that says
this is the place.

REMEMBERING A MAINE SHORE

Deliver me ten million
glacial rocks
and I'll make you a shore.

Let me spill them
between land and sea.

Hills can look down on them.
Waves slap against their
dark grey turrets.

But I'll have the weight
to snap the Atlantic rhythm
into heads of foam,
shudder the fir roots
in mute abeyance.

Come along,
sit on a flat, worn, boulder,
dangle toes, lift up head,
feel west wind dry
what east wind soaks.

Give me the parts
and I'll contrive you
a blessed whole.

It's years since
I've been home
and my heart
needs the exercise.

HOW THE NEWS GETS TO ME

Luckily the news is in newsprint,
the photos, reproductions,
its byline not my own.
At worst, I get a little ink on my fingers.
At best, I solve the crossword
or the home team wins a game.

And thankfully, it's on the radio
while I'm on my way to work,
coming through the speaker,
no bombs, no earthquakes,
just a charismatic, harmless voice.

And the news gathers
like teamwork
around the water-cooler
or sits amiably at the table
in the coffee room.
Did you hear? What about?
And then there was...

And even at night,
the news retains
that six degrees of separation...
handsome host,
charming weather-girl,
no hair out of place,
no wrinkle in the dress,
a stranger on the spot

in Iraq, Afghanistan or downtown Detroit,
and a camera-man I can't see.

Could I endure the news
if just for once I had to live it?
That's when the commercial cuts in.
With the right pills,
the best after-shave,
the consummate beer,
I won't have to.

GUY AT THE DOOR

A care package of wine
pressed to my chest,
in fading light,
at your door, begging you to open –
because it all just keeps piling up, that's why,
and I wail
or I tickle my heart with a knife blade,
or I compare you to some woman from before
but memory is such a faithless lover.

I am sorry if the fire went out.
Or you flipped a coin and I lost.
Or it just isn't my turn.
Or I climb up on the shoulders of much better men,
But I've been down in the gutter and hacking,
and dying like the wind,
and sleeping in a fifty-five-gallon drum,
scribbling on random paper just who I am,
and, in a ridiculously unsafe place,
shouting to the world "Come get me!"
gagging on my own green bile,
while the world hammers my head.

No, I don't bring heavy artillery.
Nor spells from the book of black arts.
I came up with mmmm.
You'll have to take it from there.
And as much as I climbed your stairs,
I'm willing to climb down.

I'll even lie down.
Offer you my throat.
Or my wallet.
Or even my regrets.
If you'd only let me in.
It's been six months after all.

Yes, I've walked past your house more than once.
I've dressed like a fancy man.
Or as the kind that comes and goes.
I've loaded up on good advice.
And some pills to swallow in case of recklessness.

No more dark pit, you understand.
Not when it all comes tumbling down on me.
And smells like the world.
I'm like an army that wants to take back its country.
Though there's no more violence in me.
Just inhaling, exhaling.
I could even provide shelter.
I'm made of the stuff.
And, who knows,
some sweet midnight,
I could smother you in a silent pouring of sincerity.
Imagine that.
A loving banquet for the ages.
A new broom sweeping away sad human soil.

So that's why I'm knocking.
Meanwhile, my attitude is warming up
with what I know to be the truth.
How I finally have a grip on things.
And I won't snap and, even if I did,

I'd give you plenty of warning.
So allow me one word.
One glass of wine.
My wings are plucked.
Even my dreams no longer fly.
They take cabs everywhere.
No more drab,
no more dust in swirls,
just prop me up,
let me stay indoors,
out of the grim assembly line.

Lady, you live in my thoughts.
So much hair and just enough.
A face full of the word "because."
Because only you can put my remnants back together.
Only you can un-curdle the smoke in my brain.
Only you can bend me to your shape,
float me on your current.

I realize a fine speech is out of the question.
Just pretend you had sense enough to dig me up,
take me in out of the stink and the worthlessness,
tinker with veins of life and love to start them flowing again.
And please tell me, have I covered everything.
The wine, the evening rolling in, the knock on the door.
It doesn't even matter if you're home or not.
I'm on your front step.
It's the only threshold left to me.

A KISS BY THE FROZEN RIVER

There's still a current only we can't
see it. Listen and you may hear
but the ice is as thick and cold
as any liar. The world is frozen
solid, it says.

But no, the days
still get through. And people
make it across the biting wasteland.
We're on the banks of what used
to be a river. But it flows
no different than in the rollicking
days of spring. Even in Winter,
it comes down from the mountain
to quench a distant thirsty sea.

We take our current any way
we can. Even buried deep, it follows
its own volition. I'm chilled to
the bone but the feeling flows
like blood. You grip my gloved hand.
We'll reach the mouth any day now.

THE MISSING AND THE FOUND

There are men still scouring the woods
for a young boy missing years ago.
It's a ritual, a passion, an obsession, for some.
For others, it's just something to do
on a warm, clear weekend.
That's the background to our story.
That's the familiar footfall
to our daily lives, the arguments,
the kisses, the meals, the games
of badminton in the backyard,
even the trips to the bathroom.
The family may hold together
only for the fact that we all share the same name
but I like to think that it's the hunters
stomping through the pine forest
that do it for us,
their caring, in all its shapes and guises,
gluing together the homes they pass
in their inveterate seeking,
the ones that haven't lost a child to the deep,
forbidding woods,
that don't require a search party
for the boy who, under pressure,
admits his mother love
or the other for whom there's no quest required,
merely a swift hand to the rear end
when he shoots the BB gun at passing cars.
They may never locate the body.
Maybe there isn't one to find.

But there's bodies aplenty in our house.
And when there's people out looking,
then we're never done finding.

AT THE REUNION

We form in packs,
not the cliques of thirty years before
but new cliques,
expensive suits, cheap suits,
and the few who didn't care to know
the event was semi-formal.

It's no longer jocks versus geeks,
cheerleaders versus spotty faces,
but success, doing well enough,
just getting by and thank God
for the cheese tray and those
flaky, rolled, unnamable, hot things.

The ones whose family contacts
assured them the top rung
welcome in the ones who made it
on their own initiatives.
Those who failed, despite
all their advantages,
hang out with the guy
in overalls who's living on the streets.

We're all surprised at how
easy the remembering is.
The taking stock is harder
but even that's accelerated
by the wine.
One glance around the room
and it all comes flooding back,
it all keeps moving forward.

VISITING THE OLD SCHOOL ROOM

The room looks down on the playground
with its stone frogs for leaping
and old rusty slide.
The desks are ancient,
carved with many generations of initials.

They still boast inkwells,
and holes to keep a quill pen quiet.
What weapons they must have made.
I can just imagine stabbing a sharp steel nib
into the fleshy right arm
of the annoying kid beside me.

I wonder how children ever wrote
on such uneven wood.
Every knothole, each gouged letter,
is an enemy of carefully wrought script.
And, according to my grandmother,
in those days, neatness was all.

Huge radiators line both walls.
Chalk dust, older than the dinosaurs
fills the cracks in the gray slate blackboard.
Latin was taught here by nuns
who figured it for their native tongue.

My grandmother was of the jazz age
but, within these walls,
the times are mediaeval.

I nudge a globe but it doesn't turn.
Why does that not surprise me?

THIS EMPTY HOUSE

I inhabit an empty house.
Except for the spiders
that carry on these silent conversations
with the dust.
And the television
with its infinite cast of characters
and passing traffic
that never misses an opportunity
to shine its lights on bare walls.
There's nothing here
to keep a person truly occupied.
That's why no one's ever moved in.
The thump of the radiator is not a person.
Nor is the floorboard creak
or the rattle of windows.
Or the sparse array of food in the cupboards,
the cans of beer in the refrigerator.
Nor the lumpy couch.
Nor the ratty carpet.
The books might have been once
but it takes a reader
to invite the characters in.
No, this house is as vacant
as a poor man's pockets.
The clothes in the closet don't count.
Nor does the razor in the bathroom.
The bed is solid enough
but it's not human.
Likewise the shadows

and their near relatives,
the photos on the mantel.
Not even my presence
can alter the fact –
there's no one living here.
So don't bother to knock. Or call.
I've tried that myself
and I got no answer.

POISE

The night's no longer anything but night,
death's anonymous, the skyline breeze kills
the first drop of summer rain. The greenest
of meadows meets the blackest of shadows and
a bird drops dead at the thought of it.

My life struggles to be always near the sea.
My heart mistakes a wave for a flame. My thoughts
are pebbles salt-washed into sheen. The
light sometimes stops here in my hair. I forget
I sometimes step on driftwood, that my excuses

are the sounds of rotten timber cracking. The
moon has broken up with passion. The stars are
an unholy, unhealthy lot. All that gleam,
weary with a billion years getting here.
My blood is mud. My eyes a glittering target

for the fullness of the window lights.
The streets are armpits mistaken for nests.
The flash cars are inaccessible dreams. The
ones I drive are like plowshares cutting against
the beggar's graveyards. Women crack open

long closed-drawers. My underwear is like something
planted years ago, that never grew, that barely
sustained. Sometimes, a head rests on my elbow
and it grows into a tumor. That's the night right
there. A cancerous face, its eye-lids closed in peace.

THE STRANGERS IN YOUR ROOM

I could be the mailman for all you know.
What's this? No letters.
Or maybe I'm the baker, the one
who used to leave the newly-cooked loaf
on the top step beside the milk bottles.
And no, I'm not the milk-man either.
You surely don't believe that I'm the teacher,
the strict one I used to hear so much about.
Besides, she was a woman.
You do know the difference, don't you.
You'd rather, I'm sure, that I was an old fishing pal,
come to the door with creel and poles,
with bait enough to last a week,
and saying, "Come on Charlie, the trout are biting."
I'm anyone but me I figure.
You stare like I could be familiar,
but then you turn away.
I'm just one more flower in a vase, one more
photograph you shake your head at, one more
half-eaten cinnamon roll on a plate.
Or maybe I'm your father, the one
who didn't know you from a quilt pattern
in his last days.
You told me once how cruel that was.
So I'm cruelty.
Glad to know you. Glad you don't know me.

AT THE TRAFFIC LIGHT

I will not react
like someone who needs
to be some place
five minutes ago.

I'll bite my tongue
and the horn
will do the same.

I will make allowances
for all that is going on in the life
of the back of the head
in the car in front of me.

What if he's just been diagnosed
with fourth stage cancer
or he's lost his job of thirty years
or his wife has left him.

Yes, the light is green
and he hasn't budged
but who'd want to go
in such circumstances.

I will curb my natural
aggressive behavior.
I won't shake my fist
or scream obscenities.

He's a fellow human being
and deserving of my respect.

He did not ask to be the car
ahead of me at this traffic light.
But, if he had,
I would have screamed emphatically
"No!"

LEAVING WORK, THREE HOURS BE-FORE HER EXPECTED ARRIVAL

On busy sidewalks, crowds go about their business.
They can't know what's in my head. Raining,
they dash for shelter, clear and their faces shine.

I dash, I shine, and the weather doesn't come into it.
They think I'm participating: look in store window,
catch bus, slap brief-case against thigh.

But I'm lighting lamps along the front path to a door.
I'm making a room ready, gathering information
someone else will need to know.

Strangers jostle and imagine that I jostle back.
They cough, believe the germs they spread are
non-negotiable. But I bump into nothing but anxiety.

I don't catch a thing that I don't already have.
It's on their minds, I'm sure, that we've all
done this a thousand times or more:

commuted, shopped, dined, even people-watched.
But I'm turning a bed down, I'm starting the coffee
maker, I'm on edge, waiting for the door bell's chime.

It's the ultimate misunderstanding: the immigrant of
soon joins the swell of now's population.
You'll be home tonight. But today's not expecting you.

SCRIBBLE NIGHT

Why do I remember you
absentmindedly scribbling on a napkin
more than anything else about you?
In my mind,
your hand is dancing with its partner of a pen,
scratching, scraping the flimsy ballroom floor.
Shapes are emerging
like they don't with love or anger.
Is that a face? Is it a cow? A dragon?
Why can't I fit the hugs into my head,
strolls along the beach,
waves gladly tilling in our footsteps.
I can see the restaurant
but there's no waiters,
no one's serving any food.
There's just you, head bent,
hair falling across your face,
a long silence between us,
and your fingers darting this way, that way,
squiggles falling from them
like rain from gray clouds,
though I don't remember it ever raining on you,
or clouds blackening you with shadow.
The farther away I live from that time,
the more disconnected I am from the emotion.
Maybe there was none.
Maybe the boredom was the great silence
that sent you doodling,
that had me looking because I had to focus somewhere.

Who would have thought a falling apart
would have its diagram,
a feeling not quite something,
a drawing not quite anything.

FOUR YEARS INTO THE RELATIONSHIP

It's the same street from the day before.
Same cars cruising down it.
Same heads hanging out the windows
like overripe grapes on vines.
If time was measured in Fords
parked in driveways, red curtains drawn,
rusted numbers on houses,
roses withering in gardens,
scrap metal overflowing dumpsters,
my watch would say yesterday.
I picked up the newspaper from your front lawn,
refused to give the game away
by looking at the date.
It couldn't have been today's...
nothing was today's.
But what if it was from a week ago,
from last year, that yellowing
broadsheet with its even more yellowed news.
I knocked on the door
like a busted clock
thunking instead of chiming.
You opened it like
it had never been closed,
greeted me as if I'd been here
all the time,
then kissed my cheek,
reclaiming your lips
from where you'd left them last time.

RIGHTING A RAFT

There's this myth
that it was our entire family
that tied ropes around
the capsized raft,
knotting figure eights
to the frame's downstream side.
But no, it was just me
and a few of my outdoor friends.

The story goes that my mother,
sisters and I struggled back
into the water, pulled hard
against the rocking flow,
while my father dug in
behind us, like a rock
in whirlpool foam.
But it was just buddies who
fooled the current into righting it.

What do you want me to say?
That every tough job we licked
together just because we lived
under one roof?
No, the confinement, the closeness,
worked against us.
Harmony, everyone doing our bit...
tell that to the wall-cracks,
the tear-stained pillows.

There's another myth
that our familiarity, our hostilities.
tipped the damn water-craft over
in the first place.
Now that I can believe.

UNLIKE THE HOME WHERE I WAS RAISED

How neat everything is, like no one lives here.
No dirt. No dust. Nothing crumpled. Look at
the beds. Not a crease or sheet edge showing. There's
no such thing as sleep apparently. And not one stain
in kitchen sink, on cabinet. How orderly the world
would be if nobody ate. Her eyes beam. She's
proud of floors that deny there ever was a human footprint.

But you assure me, people were actually raised in this house.
You, your sister, for two. Maybe you slept outside
beneath the rose petals. And did you dine on tree
bark? Did aphids tuck you in at night?

We sit at the edge of a covered sofa. She sets our
coffee on coasters wide as frisbees. When muffins crumble
in our fingers, it's as if the world is doing the same.
A vacuum cleaner stands by. We are the villains of
the piece. Hoover's her Young Lochinvar. "She
really did love us," you say, more to yourself than
to me. "She changed our diapers, wiped our muddy
faces." As we leave, her lips brush your cheeks.
Not to plant a kiss but to mop up an old one.

THE RIGHT ONE

If she pushes a wheelbarrow load
of rocks up a steeply sloping field

or she stands in a bog, halfway up her legs,
lifts her dress to go even deeper

or she laughs as she curses
at the manure that cakes her shoes.

Or maybe if she's not afraid of a snake
or kicks a rat across the mud floor of the barn,

you'll love her. Forget about oils and lipstick.
If she's as thrilled as you at the sight of

a cord of wood stacked neatly by the shed,
then you'll marry the woman as soon as the crop

is harvested and the coop check comes in.
You'll even have children if the rains arrive on time

and you'll love them if they've a cold, true eye
when shooting rabbits in the woods.

You'll even love God if he does something about
the northern winds, the rock heave and the twisters.

But first there has to be that feeling for yourself,
the one that you confuse with falling hog prices.

A man born to the land, you call yourself.
Well it wouldn't be the first father that didn't want you.

SECOND LOVE, LONGEST WINTER

Winter was so anxious to get here,
it roared into town late October,
on a great whoosh of Canadian wind.
The leaves were falling before
they even had a chance to change color.
The fields, still sore from harvesting,
were dumped upon by snow.
I barely had a fire lit
and it already wasn't warm enough.
The dog wanted in
the very moment he wanted out.

Kids looked up at the sky,
wondered why it had it in
for their skate-boards.
The forest hikers cursed.
The squirrels hadn't nearly enough
stored away.
Migration was stopped in its tracks,
from late-leaving robins
to retirees with their vans hardly packed
for Florida.

It was like the town, at fifty two,
clutched at its heart, dropped down dead.
Or its school football team
got its butt beat up good by some nobodies.
And Carol and I had met in spring,
fell in love over summer,

were expecting our passion
to gradually cool through the Fall.
It didn't just cool,
it chilled us instantly to the heart.
What a winter that was...
dead trees and my undying gratitude.